WONDER
A 25-DAY CHRISTMAS & ADVENT DEVOTIONAL

BY ANDY BLANKS

PUBLISHED BY YM360

TABLE of CONTENTS

Day 1	4
Day 2	5
Day 3	6
Day 4	7
Day 5	8
Day 6	9
Day 7	10
Day 8	11
Day 9	12
Day 10	13
Day 11	14
Day 12	15
Day 13	16
Day 14	17
Day 15	18
Day 16	19
Day 17	20
Day 18	21
Day 19	22
Day 20	23
Day 21	24
Day 22	25
Day 23	26
Day 24 Christmas Eve	27
Day 24 Christmas Eve (Family Devotion)	28
Day 25 Christmas Day	29
Day 25 Christmas Day (Family Devotion)	30
About The Author	31

INTRODUCTION

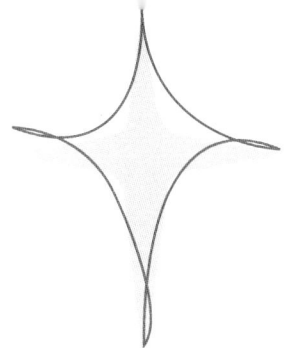

There are few things more enjoyable than watching a child open their presents on Christmas morning. The joy. The excitement. The wonder of it all. *Wonder;* what a concept. Wonder is part of what makes Christmas such a special season. What is your relationship with "wonder"? People who see the world with wonder experience their surroundings with a sort of curious surprise. To wonder is to soak up the absolute joy of a particular experience. Children display wonder at Christmas. The question is, do you?

When faced with the story of Christmas, the incredible tale of God becoming human in order to build a bridge back to Himself, do you experience wonder? Are you in awe of God's audacity? Do you marvel at His creativity? Are you overwhelmed at how HUGE His plan is?

If any of these things are true, then you are someone who knows what it means to wonder at God.

There is so much wonder contained in the Christmas story. The wonder of God's amazing birth announcement to Elizabeth and Zechariah. The wonder of Mary and Joseph's encounter with the angel. The wonder of John leaping in the womb of his mother. The wonder of the virgin birth. The wonder of the shepherds' encounter with a heavenly host. The wonder of the magi. Every single aspect of the entire incarnation narrative is saturated with wonder. We just have to see it.

The last stanza of the timeless Christmas hymn, "Joy To the World," captures this sentiment:

> *"He rules the earth with truth and grace,*
> *and makes the nations prove*
> *the glories of his righteousness,*
> *and wonders of his love."*

Remember how that song ends? We don't just sing "and wonders of his love" once. We sing it three times! The goal of this devotional is to help you remember the wonder of the love of God that we see so clearly in His relentless pursuit of His people.

May this Christmas season be a *wonderful* one.

DAY 1

DEVOTIONAL PASSAGE: ISAIAH 9:6-7

What if you walked into school this morning, and your PE teacher looked at you and said, "Hey! By the end of the day, you're going to be $20 richer. Count on it." You would probably laugh uncomfortably, all the while thinking to yourself that the constant whistle blowing has finally rattled something loose in his brain. But then, what if at some point during the day, a friend walks up to you and says, "This is crazy, I know, but I want you to have this," and presses a $20 bill in your hand. What would you think of your PE teacher then? You'd probably be shocked, amazed, freaked out, and maybe even thankful that you're $20 richer. In short, you would look at your PE teacher with wonder.

Here's the cool thing: God did something similar to this, except about a million times more wonderful. Take a second and read Isaiah 9:6-7. Isaiah 9:6-7 was written by Isaiah, one of the most important prophets in the Bible. Isaiah was sharing the words God had given to Isaiah for His people. The problem was that the Israelites, God's chosen people, had pretty much turned their backs on God. God had given them a lot of advanced warning, but they hadn't listened. So, Isaiah was warning the people that God's judgment was coming.

But the most profound thing is that even while promising His people judgment for their rebellion, God promised them hope. Isaiah 9:6-7 is God telling His people of a hopeful future in which God once and for all provides relief from the penalty of our sins. Fast forward a few hundred years, and you see this message of hope coming to life in the Christmas story. The baby God was forming in Mary's stomach? He was the same promised savior Isaiah was writing about in Isaiah 9:6-7. You want to talk about something that makes you respond in wonder? Long before God sent Jesus to this earth, He knew the plan. Jesus was always the plan! God has always known that Jesus would be the answer to a perfect relationship between God and His children, which is great news for you and me. But to see this plan come to life, Jesus had to come to earth. And that's what Christmas is all about.

THINK ABOUT THIS:

- God has had a plan to redeem you from the consequences of your sins for all eternity. How does that help you trust Him with your worries, concerns, and future?
- Take a moment to reflect on the wonder of a prophecy made hundreds of years before Jesus' birth that was perfectly true in Christ. Thank God for His creative, relentless, awe-inspiring love for you and the world.

DAY 2

DEVOTIONAL PASSAGE: MATTHEW 1:1-17

Yesterday we looked at the wonder of prophecy and how amazing it is that God could make a promise that would come true hundreds of years later. (Well, it's amazing to us; for God, it's prety normal.) Today is going to be another look at a similar move by God. But this one is really, really personal.

Take a moment and read Matthew 1:1-17. Yes, read every single name. All the easy ones. And all the weird ones. Finished? Hopefully, you recognized some of the names. Abraham. Isaac. Joseph. David. Maybe even a few others (like Rahab, a reformed prostitute, proving that God can redeem anyone from their sins). Most of them you probably have never heard before, and that's OK. But even though you don't recognize their names, this list is super important. It's not just a strange cultural thing that would have been popular 2,000 years ago.

This list of names accomplishes a few things: it proves that Jesus is the promised Messiah, who would one day be sent to restore the Israelites. (Of course, we know that Jesus did more than just save the Israelites; through His death and resurrection, Jesus provided a way for all who will believe in Him to be saved from their sins.) Old Testament prophecy said that the Messiah would come from the line of David. Look back at verse 7. Whose name do you see?

But, among other things, this list doesn't simply prove that Jesus' lineage was what it should be. It proves that God works through people. It proves that every life matters. This list is full of people who were going about their lives, living as faithfully as possible. While we don't know for sure, it's safe to say that the overwhelming majority of them had ZERO idea that one of their ancestors would be God's promised Son. Most of them were ordinary people living ordinary lives. And yet, thousands of years later, we read their names.

There is so much wonder in this! Your life works much the same way. You have no idea what God is doing in and through you, but you can know for sure that God is using you to advance His Kingdom.

THINK ABOUT THIS:

- In what ways does your life function to the world around you as a testimony of the "realness" of God?
- Is there anything in your life that is an obstacle to your wonder? What would it take for you to remove that obstacle so you can see this Christmas season with open eyes?

DAY 3

DEVOTIONAL PASSAGE: LUKE 1:5-7

Some of the biggest wonder-producing moments come when we are shocked out of our expectations.

Read Luke 1:5-7. In this passage, we meet Zechariah and Elizabeth. These two people are extremely important to the Christmas story and in Jesus' overall ministry. But today, let's focus on what we know about them from these verses. In verse 5, we discover that Zechariah was a priest. This means that he would have represented his people before God in the Temple. He would have led them in worship and in making sacrifices and offerings. We know he was married to Elizabeth. In verse 6, we see that Elizabeth and Zechariah were godly people. They were meticulous in following God and His ways. But in verse 7, we learn something really sad.

In verse 7, we see that they had no child. When Luke's original audience read this verse after reading verses 5-6, they would have been caught off guard. Why? Because in this period, if you weren't able to have children, it was thought that God was judging you because of some sin in your life. Yikes!

Spoiler alert: Zechariah and Elizabeth would miraculously become pregnant with a child. That child would be the man we know as John the Baptist (more on that later). What we see from this story is God working in ways that defy our expectations. This childless couple? They would miraculously become the parents of a crucial partner in Jesus' ministry. But not yet. God wasn't quite ready for them to be blown away by His amazing plan for them. In the meantime, they were left to deal with unmet dreams and frustrated expectations. And yet, they did so faithfully. There is much for us to learn from them, isn't there?

THINK ABOUT THIS:

- What is something you wanted badly that God didn't choose to provide for you?
- Zechariah and Elizabeth stayed faithful even though God had not yet granted their desires. What can you learn from their example?

DEVOTIONAL PASSAGE: LUKE 1:8-17

Do you remember the last time that you were on the receiving end of a really great surprise? Did you make the "I'm so surprised" face? You know the look: eyebrows up, eyes wide, mouth open. Maybe you put your hands to your face. There's nothing like a good surprise.

Guess what? In every surprise, there is a little bit of wonder. There is a little bit of that child-like joy, a happiness that comes from the sudden, unexpected goodness of it all. In today's devotion, you're going to see a guy get surprised in about the most fantastic way possible.

Read Luke 1:8-17. In the passage you just read, Zechariah found out he would be receiving the thing he and his wife had most longed for. In their old age, the couple would have a son. Zechariah had to be surprised. But look back at verses 14-17. This was no ordinary baby. This child, who would grow up to be John the Baptist, would play a significant role in God's rescue plan to save people from their sins. So not only did Zechariah and Elizabeth have their prayers answered, but they were also answered most miraculously.

"Do not be afraid, for your prayer has been heard." Zechariah would be excused if his first response was fear. It's not every day an angel pops up in the middle of your work. But the angel told him to be happy, not afraid. Why? Because God was on the move, preparing the world to receive His Son, Jesus, and Zechariah, and Elizabeth had a role to play.

As you think about Zechariah and Elizabeth, ask yourself how their story impacts your story. God is able and willing to work through you to shake up the world for His glory. Pray to God and ask Him to use you in extraordinary ways, just like He used Zechariah, Elizabeth, and eventually, their son John. And then get ready to wonder at how He will answer you.

THINK ABOUT THIS:

- Would you say that you expect God to do amazing things in your life? Why or why not?
- What if you were to truly pray that God would work through you to do mighty things for His glory and BELIEVED that He would? How would this change the way you see God and your life?

DAY 5

DEVOTIONAL PASSAGE: LUKE 1:18-25

When was the last time someone in your world did something dumb and got made fun of for it? If you're honest, this happens a lot. Most of it is harmless; you drop your tray in the lunchroom, and while everyone laughs, and while it may not feel great, it's over and done with soon enough. You move on, and it's forgotten. But what happens when that mistake is a "big" one?

You know the cycle: a person makes a mistake in something they say or do, and suddenly it's a free-for-all. Everyone is making fun of them. Your private snaps are blowing up, and maybe some public ones too. People talk about it in the locker room and on the bus, and the offending person is made to feel small or stupid. They become the butt of the joke. They are, in essence, shamed. To make themselves look bigger, people work hard to make others look smaller every chance they get.

Read Luke 1:18-25. Pay special attention to 24-25. The beautiful thing about this encounter is that God is in the "shame removing" business. In Elizabeth's culture, infertility was seen as a sign of God's punishment for sin. So, Elizabeth would have carried around this shame her entire life, even though she had done nothing to deserve her infertility. But God miraculously removed her shame, and He did it for countless people in the New Testament. God is all about taking away the shame from our lives.

Wrapped up in the Christmas story is the story of Zechariah and Elizabeth. Two ordinary folks who were dealing with their own issues. But God acted miraculously in their lives to both weave the big-picture story of His plan to send His Son to rescue the world and to personally remove their pain and shame. This is what God does, time and time again. There is wonder in this—a ton of it. If you are dealing with the shame of sin, take heart: Jesus is uniquely capable of taking away this shame.

THINK ABOUT THIS:

- What causes you to feel shame?
- Is shame keeping you from feeling as close to God as you want to?
- Make it a point to spend some time in prayer, asking God to help you feel free of the shame of your brokenness. Ask Him to remind you of His great love for you and His desire to forgive our sins

DEVOTIONAL PASSAGE: LUKE 1:26-29

Read Luke 1:26-29. There are a few things that we can discover about Mary here. First, she was from Nazareth in Galilee. Luke's original readers would have know this meant that Mary was not from a big city. Nazareth was considered a small, kind of backwoods town. So, the original audience might have drawn some conclusions about Mary based on where she lived. Second, she was a virgin engaged to be married to Joseph. In other words, she had never been with a man sexually. Mary was morally upright. She was also young. Most scholars believe Mary was only around 14 or 15 years old at the time. But above all, Mary was confused. And who could blame her?

Put yourself in Mary's shoes. One day you're minding your business. The next, an angel sent from the Lord is giving you a message. "Favored one"? What in the world was that all about? "A message from God to me"? Can you imagine how confused she must have been? Verse 29 says Mary was troubled and was trying to figure all of this out.

We can relate to Mary, can't we? While God may not choose to have you parent His Son, God does have plans for your life. Specific and important plans. Sometimes these plans may confuse you. If they do, don't worry. You're in good company. Mary was confused, too. But Mary ultimately trusted God's plan (more on this tomorrow). That's our challenge as well.

When God leads you down a road you're unsure of, know beyond a shadow of a doubt that it's exactly where you're supposed to be. Trust, and stay true. And keep your eyes open. You're God's plan to share His name with the world.

THINK ABOUT THIS:

- Can you think of a time when you knew God was working in your life, but you didn't know exactly what He was doing? What emotions did you feel?
- If you aren't aware of God working in or through you, what does that say about your faith? (Here's a hint: God is always present and always at work. If you can't feel it, the issue is not with God.)
- Take a moment to pray today that God will help you have a clear vision to see what He is doing in your life.

DAY 7

DEVOTIONAL PASSAGE: LUKE 1:30-33

Think about what it's like to wait for something you are really excited about. The days pass by like weeks. You go through about a million different emotions. Anxious. Apathetic. Frustrated. Resigned. And then . . . boom! The day you've waited for is here!

Read Luke 1:30-33. For us to understand the news Mary received, we need a little background info. Sometime around a thousand years before Mary's time, King David ruled Israel. Things were swell, for the most part. Then, David died, and his son Solomon was king. And things were awesome. Really awesome. Israel was at the height of its time as a nation. They had money. They had power. They had relative peace. Things were rocking. But then, Solomon had to go and mess everything up.

Solomon turned away from God. And as a result, Israel would be split into two kingdoms after his death: a northern and a southern kingdom. God sent the prophets to warn Israel to turn back to God. But they didn't listen. Within about 500 years, God allowed both the northern and southern kingdoms to be destroyed. But all during this time, God continued to send a message of hope. He continued to promise that a Messiah would come. God promised to send His Son to be the hope of Israel and the world.

So you see, the Jews had been waiting for the Messiah for hundreds of years. Hundreds. And then one day . . . boom! An angel is telling Mary that the Messiah is here and that SHE will be His mother! Unbelievable! Can you imagine what she must have felt like hearing the angel's words? Those words describe a powerful, miraculous ruler who would deliver people from their sins. Jesus would be the rescuer of the world. And He would be Mary's son. If that's not the most wonderful birth announcement ever written, I don't know what is.

THINK ABOUT THIS:

- Re-read verses 32-33. What description of Jesus most stands out to you?
- How has the good news of Jesus changed your life? Have you ever thought about the answer to that question?
- Is there someone in your life who needs to hear that Jesus is the king, come to redeem all people from their sins? What's keeping you from telling them?

DAY 8

DEVOTIONAL PASSAGE: LUKE 1:34-38

There is wonder when what seemed impossible suddenly turns possible. Those videos where the Marine who had been serving overseas shows up and surprises a loved one? They are so surprised because they believe the reunion to be impossible. People go nuts when they watch someone on a skateboard or a bike nail a previously un-tried trick for the first time. Why? Because what they thought was impossible just became possible. We marvel when these kinds of things happen—we WONDER. Our minds are blown, and the way we once looked at things is changed.

Read Luke 1:34-38. Have you ever prayed for something you thought could never happen only to see it happen? Have you ever seen God "open a door" you thought was closed? Have you ever watched God blow away your human-based understanding with a God-sized movement? When the impossible became possible?

Mary did. Mary watched God do the impossible. She watched Him defy the laws of nature. But before she saw the miracle, she doubted the Miracle Maker.

Look back at verse 34. For a moment, even face-to-face with an angel, Mary had an attack of humanity. "How can this happen?" Mary knew how babies were made, and she knew for a fact she wasn't a candidate! But Mary forgot one thing. The rules that she knew governed the creation of life? The process she was sure she had not been a part of? Mary forgot that God set those rules in place. God created the process! He can work outside the process when He chooses.

Never forget: Nothing is impossible with God.

THINK ABOUT THIS:

· Is your vision of God too small because you put limitations on Him? How might your relationship with God be different if you saw Him for who He was?
· Take a few minutes and praise God for His ability to constantly surprise us and keep us in awe. Ask for God to show you ways He has made the impossible "possible" in your life.

DAY 9

DEVOTIONAL PASSAGE: LUKE 1:38

Today we're going to spend a little more time on Mary. The goal is to look closely at her situation to get a sense of wonder for what God did in and through her. Re-read Luke 1:38. Put yourself in Mary's shoes. You're minding your business, doing whatever a 1st-century Jewish girl would have done on any given day. We don't know what Mary was doing. But whatever it was, suddenly it was forgotten.

In the middle of what we can imagine might have been a normal day, an angel appeared. Let that sink in for a minute. You're Mary, and you're doing what you do. And then, boom, Gabriel's in your living room! It's no wonder the first thing he said was basically, "Hey Mary! It's all good! Don't freak out. We're cool!" We can only imagine how frightened we'd be if we were all of a sudden face-to-face with an angel.

But maybe the most unsettling thing was Gabriel's message.

Imagine being told you were going to be pregnant. Keep in mind that you're not married, so this message has its problems. Oh, and one more thing: the baby won't be your fiancé's. And it won't be conceived by human means. It will be God's child, His Son, the long-awaited Messiah, promised for centuries. How's that for an announcement?

Mary was confused, for sure. And not surprisingly. Can you imagine trying to grasp a message like this? What would her friends say? Who would believe her? What would her husband-to-be think? Would he believe her? And what did it mean that God's Son would live and grow inside here? The questions must have flooded Mary's mind.

But her response was pretty amazing. In verse 38, we see Mary do something powerful in its simplicity: she surrendered. "I'm the Lord's servant, and I'm on board." Her obedience cleared the way for her to be one of the major players in the greatest story ever told.

THINK ABOUT THIS:

- Why is it so difficult to surrender our lives to God's leading?
- What does our hesitation say about our level of trust in God?
- Do you ever think about what God has planned for you that you miss out on because you want to be in control of your life instead of surrendering it to God?

DAY 10

DEVOTIONAL PASSAGE: MATTHEW 1:18-25

What is the opposite of wonder? Weird question, right? Maybe there isn't even an answer to it. Or maybe, there is more than one answer. What if you were told that the opposite of wonder was disappointment? That sort of makes sense. If wonder is a sense of joy-filled excitement and disappointment is when our expectations don't match reality, then they are opposites.

Read Matthew 1:18-25. Joseph found himself in the mother of all unmet expectations. He was engaged to Mary, the girl he loved. The couple had correctly chosen to wait until marriage to engage in sexual relations. And yet, Joseph was met with some news that must have sounded absolutely nuts to his ears: his sweet fiancé Mary was pregnant. And if that wasn't enough, she claimed it was God who had conceived the baby inside of her. As we'll look at it more closely tomorrow, Joseph ultimately made the right call. He eventually believed Mary. All was well. But do you ever wonder if he still struggled a bit with unmet expectations?

Sure, Joseph was a miraculous, amazing part of God's plan to rescue humankind from their sins. But do you ever wonder how Joseph felt about this? Maybe he was shy and simple. Maybe he didn't want the pressure of being part of God's plan. His expectations of a "normal" marriage went away pretty quickly. Do you wonder if he was disappointed at first? Before he grasped what it meant to be the earthly father of God's Son? To Joseph's credit, he rolled with it. He adjusted his expectations, got used to his "new normal," and devoted himself to Mary and Jesus.

God will often do things differently than we want or expect. We can let this derail us, or we can trust God and go with His flow. We know what Joseph chose. What would you choose?

THINK ABOUT THIS:

- Think of a time when God did something for you or through you that was awesome, but that completely went against your expectations. How did it make you feel?
- How can our expectations sometimes be an excuse to do things the same old way we've always done them?
- Are you brave enough to pray and ask God to blow away your expectations of Him and how He wants to use you?

DAY 11

DEVOTIONAL PASSAGE: MATTHEW 1:24-25

It's hard to suspend our disbelief. What does that mean? It means, as human beings, we struggle with believing something when everything in us says not to believe it. We're conditioned this way by the world around us. When every celebrity is Photoshopped to perfection, and every seemingly random video is actually scripted and produced, who can blame us if we have a hard time believing things? Especially things that seem too crazy to be true.

Read Matthew 1:24-25. Think about Joseph. Joseph and Mary were to be married, but Mary became pregnant. Now, Matthew lets us know that it was the Holy Spirit's work. But, look at Joseph's response: He was going to break off the marriage.

Mary told Joseph about the angel, but for whatever reason, Joseph didn't seem willing to believe her. (Or maybe he did but was unwilling to face the ridicule of his friends and neighbors.) Matthew tells us that Joseph was a good man. But who could have blamed him for wanting out of the marriage? Imagine if your fiancé told you she was pregnant with God's baby. Would you be quick to suspend your disbelief?

Thankfully, God wasn't done with Joseph. He sent an angel to tell Joseph that Mary was telling the truth. It must have been bittersweet for Joseph. He must have felt excited to learn what was happening, but maybe a twinge of shame that he didn't stick with Mary in the first place.

The coolest thing about Joseph? His willingness to trust that God would make it all work out. Joseph heard the angel's message and essentially said, "OK. I'm in. I don't understand all this, but I'll trust God." As Christ-followers, we're called to have the same trust in God. We might not always understand where God is leading us. But like Joseph, we can trust that God is in control. He knows where He's taking us. And that's all that matters.

THINK ABOUT THIS:

- How does trust in God help you navigate the many decisions about the future that you're facing or will be facing soon?
- What does your level of trust in God say about how well you know Him? What can you do to grow in your trust in God?

DAY 12

DEVOTIONAL PASSAGE: LUKE 1:39-45

When remarkable things happen to us, it's only natural that we approach these situations with wonder. And when we are in awe about something really cool, we tend to share the good news. Think of how weird it would be for you to have something truly amazing happen to you, and you told no one. No snapping your friends. Nothing on TikTok or Instagram. Nothing. This situation isn't likely to happen, is it? Good news just seems better when we have someone to share it with.

If you have a second, think of a particularly exciting event you've recently experienced. Write it down on the left side of the box below. Then, on the right side, write down the first three people you told.

Take a moment and read Luke 1:39-45. Just like you went and shared your exciting news with the people you listed above, Mary couldn't wait to tell her cousin Elizabeth of the news. Whether Mary knew of Elizabeth's news or not, we don't know for sure. But the cool thing is that BOTH women had exciting news to share. The coolest thing of all is that Elizabeth's excitement bubbled over in a Holy Spirit-fueled burst of joy that affirmed the angel's message to Mary: the baby in Mary's stomach was indeed the Messiah, God's Son.

Part of the idea of approaching Christmas with a sense of wonder is to ask how our wonder changes our life. Would you say that you are still excited about the work God is doing in and through you? Or have you lost your sense of wonder when it comes to your faith? God IS working in you. Every day. And He is working through you to reach the world in His name. Don't fall into the trap of getting so used to this fact that you take it for granted. Take a tip from Mary and Elizabeth. Embrace your sense of wonder for what God is doing.

THINK ABOUT THIS:

- What obstacles keep you from being more aware of the work God is doing in your life?
- What can you do to minimize these obstacles and make room for more excitement about what God is doing?
- Spend a few moments in prayer to God, thanking Him for all He continues to do in and through you. Ask Him to lead you to a place where you can express joy and excitement over His role in your life.

DAY 13

DEVOTIONAL PASSAGE: LUKE 1:46-56

Look around you. What in your life brings you joy? This isn't "church answer" time. It's OK to say something like, "my car," or "my family," or even "cheerleading," or "football," or "my guitar." Many things in our lives make us happy. Some of them we think about often (like family or friends). Some of them we may kind of take for granted (like food or our health).

Read Luke 1:46-56. Mary wasn't about to take anything for granted. Again, she had just had a pretty amazing interaction. So, she headed over to see her cousin, Elizabeth. Elizabeth had some pretty cool news of her own: she was pregnant with her first child when most women her age had one foot in the grave. (Elizabeth would give birth to John the Baptist.) When Mary and Elizabeth saw each other and shared their news, Mary burst into a meaningful song of thankfulness.

One of the truths about our relationship with God is that He is our provider. He is the giver of good things. He is the source of all your blessings: your health, your life, your shelter, your food, and so on. Sure, God might not literally pay your family's mortgage each month or put gas in your car. But the money your family earns? The job your mom or dad has? Maybe even the job you have? It's yours through God's grace. All good things come from God.

Mary seemed to have a firm grasp on this. Do you? Are you in the habit of realizing what God has given you and then making sure He hears your thankfulness? It starts with stepping back and seeing that God has given you more than you could ever imagine. When you understand this, praise and thankfulness come naturally.

THINK ABOUT THIS:

- List out your blessings. Seriously. Do it. It's fun. Think of everything good in your life and write them down. (Or at least write a few of them.)
- Now, tell God thank you. No, really. Stop and thank God for giving you all of these things.
- Why do you think an awareness of what you have and an attitude of thankfulness is so vital to a healthy relationship with God?

DAY 14

DEVOTIONAL PASSAGE: LUKE 1:57-66

Take a moment and read John 1:57-62. Elizabeth is an older woman, way past her child-birthing years. We've already talked about what it means to her reputation that God has decided to bless her in this way. It is a true miracle. And when we look at verse 58, the people's reactions reflect this. People are pumped and are praising God as a result of this miraculous new thing that has happened. But then, we watch as their reaction changes a bit.

Tension enters the narrative at verse 59. When Elizabeth names the boy John, just as the angel had instructed her, people freak out. The people turn to what they know best: tradition and custom. They essentially said, "Whoa, whoa, whoa! You don't have anyone in your family named John. Why not name him after his dad?" And not bothering to even listen to Elizabeth, they go to chat with Zechariah about it. Maybe they thought he'd be the kind of guy to uphold tradition.

Now, read verses 62-66 (remember that Zechariah has been unable to talk for months due to his initial disbelief that God would bless him with a son). Notice that all the folks who were like, "that's not the way we do it around here," got put in their place. Zechariah supported Elizabeth and God and told the people the boy would DEFINITELY be called John. His boldness was backed up with God giving him his voice back. The people had to know something new and amazing was happening, and it shattered their understanding of "it's just how things are done."

We can't always see when God is doing big, God-sized things. We get hung up on the way things have always been. The idea is to begin to look for God to be God. Enlarge your expectations and embrace the wonder of it all. Don't box God in. Don't try to make Him fit your human-sized perspective. Look for God to do huge, awesome, amazing things. And get ready to join the work He is already doing.

THINK ABOUT THIS:

- Do you try to make God safe and predictable? Do you try to box Him in? If so, why?
- While we can know God, which is a beautiful thing, we'll never fully understand Him. His ways are too deep and grand for us. This is an awesome thing. Why? Say a prayer and ask God to help you see through any old customs or traditions keeping you from pursuing Him more.

DAY 15

DEVOTIONAL PASSAGE: LUKE 1:67-80

Today we take our last look at Zechariah and Elizabeth. You may wonder why they play such an important role in the Christmas story. That's a fair question. First, it's impossible to separate John the Baptist's ministry from Jesus' ministry. John was part of God's plan from day 1. And so John's birth story is directly tied to Jesus' birth story. But there is another reason we celebrate Zechariah and Elizabeth as part of the Christmas narrative.

Read Luke 1:67-80. This is the continuation of the story you started yesterday, and this is Zechariah's jubilant response after seeing God keep His promise of a son. (Keep in mind, these would have been the first real words that came out of Zechariah's mouth for months.) And in his response, we see why he has such an important role in the Christmas story. What do you see in Zechariah's words here? In verses 68-75, Zechariah gives us a super-quick overview of God's covenant promises made to His people throughout the Old Testament. Zechariah is combining what he knows about Jesus' birth to Mary and Joseph with what he has been told about his son John's life. He is putting the pieces together and realizing that something HUGE is happening. He is seeing God working the amazing plan He has always had in motion. Zechariah knows something special is about to go down.

Verses 68-69 say, "Blessed be the Lord God of Israel, for he has visited and redeemed his people and has raised up a horn of salvation for us in the house of his servant David." This is what Christmas is all about. This is what we celebrate. In Christ, God visited us. In Jesus, God raised up a path to salvation. Through Jesus' death on the cross, we can be redeemed from the penalty of our sins. And it all started with a little God-baby born in humble surroundings. This is the miracle of Christmas!

THINK ABOUT THIS:
- In your own words, summarize the meaning of Christmas.
- Why is it so easy to miss the meaning of Christmas as we go through this busy holiday season?
- What can you do to ensure that you don't lose sight of what Christmas is truly about?

DAY 16

DEVOTIONAL PASSAGE: LUKE 2:1-7

Wonder is a cool characteristic to have. Want to know another one? Confidence. Think about it: confidence is when you expect a certain outcome, and then you act on your expectations. In a sense, you're taking a gamble that what you THINK is going to happen will happen. Confidence is jumping out of a plane, believing the thin piece of silk in your backpack will stop your fall. Confidence is walking across a crosswalk, believing cars will stop at a red light. Confidence is going to sleep at night believing the world will be as it should be when you wake up.

Read Luke 2:1-7. While it might not seem at first like the most obvious concept in the passage you just read, the idea of confidence is pretty prominent. Where do we see it? Verse 6. Time had passed since God's revelation to Mary and Joseph. And here they were traveling to Bethlehem to be counted in the Roman census. What would happen? What would God do? Would God do as He promised? Was there another surprise in store?

We know that Mary approached all of this with great wonder. Scripture tells us that. But we wonder how confident they were. Did they doubt? How certain were they? We don't know for sure, but what we do know is this: God gave them a gift given in the form of a baby, born just as God said He would be. Fully God, the Messiah that would take away the sins of the world. Fully human, the baby wrapped in clothes, lying in a feeding trough. God came through. And because of this, Mary and Joseph could have confidence that God was who He said He was, and would accomplish what He said He would accomplish.

Wonder and confidence. Both are present when we consider the Christmas story. And maybe it takes a little of both to believe that God can and will do what He says He will do. It's taking His promises in the Bible as truth. It's living your life in a bold, vibrant faith, knowing that God will use you to grow His Kingdom. Confidence. Do you have it?

THINK ABOUT THIS:

- What has God done in your life to build your confidence in Him?
- There is a lot of uncertainty in the world these days. How does confidence in God's character affect any fears or worries you have in your life?

DAY 17

DEVOTIONAL PASSAGE: COLOSSIANS 1:15-20

Turn in your Bible or your Bible app to Colossians 1:15-20. You've just read the part in the story where Jesus was born. And you're just a few days away from celebrating His birth with Christ-followers around the world. Let's take this moment to focus on exactly who it was that was born in that manger.

Paul says that Jesus is "the image of the invisible God." When we 'see' Jesus in the Bible, we see God in human form. Paul said Jesus was "the firstborn of all creation." Jesus, the same little boy born in a manger, is the Prince of all created things. Paul says in verse 16, "For by him all things were created, in heaven and on earth, visible and invisible, whether thrones or dominions or rulers or authorities." The baby born to Mary and Joseph that night was with God when the earth was spoken into being. Paul writes that, "all things were created through him and for him." Jesus was the author of all creation. The world exists to glorify Him. In verse 17, Paul says, "And he is before all things, and in him all things hold together." The same Jesus who spent His first night in a meager stable is the unifying force that keeps all creation moving forward.

The frail newborn looking up at Mary and Joseph? Paul wrote that He is "the head of the body, the church. He is the beginning, the firstborn from the dead, that in everything he might be preeminent." This seemingly normal-looking baby whose birth angels foretold? "In him all the fullness of God was pleased to dwell."

Most importantly, the God-child we celebrate on Christmas would be the lynchpin of God's plan to rescue humanity from sin and death. Through Jesus, God would "reconcile to himself all things, whether on earth or in heaven, making peace by the blood of his cross."

THIS is the baby we celebrate! Jesus is the culmination of God's plan to redeem humankind from the separation sin causes. And maybe the most amazing thing about it all is that this very Jesus knows you and chooses to let you know Him.

THINK ABOUT THIS:

- Take some time today and simply PRAISE Jesus for who He is. Praise Him for His identity, but also for who He is to you personally.

DAY 18

DEVOTIONAL PASSAGE: LUKE 2:8-14

Have you ever been in a situation where suddenly your assumptions or thoughts about a specific person or thing were pretty much blown off the map? Maybe it was the moment you realized the little test you were "prepared" for was really an overwhelming obstacle you had no chance of conquering. Or the moment you realize that she really does like you, a lot! Or how about the moment you realize your team is completely overmatched. You get the point. There are moments of clarity where what you thought was the case may not necessarily be the case at all.

Read Luke 2:8-14. The shepherds who were in the fields outside of Bethlehem? They experienced one of those moments in a big, big way. It's safe to say that the shepherds knew God. Or they knew of Him as well as they could. They were Israelites. Their people had a rich history with God. They were, after all, God's people. But, everything they thought they knew about God and His ways was pretty much overwhelmed that night. All of a sudden, the God who was a little distant and a lot mysterious was right up in their world. In their faces!

Look at the description in verse 9: "the glory of the Lord shone around them." Can you imagine? God was no longer an abstract or impersonal force; He was real. He had broken the invisible barrier between His Kingdom and this world. And it's entirely safe to say the world was never the same. Isn't that a pretty good way to think about the Christmas story in general?

Isn't it as simple as God breaking the barrier and coming into our world? It is that simple. Yet, the power behind this simple truth is life-changing.

You are who you are today because God chose to send His Son into this world.

THINK ABOUT THIS:

- Answer this: How does Christ coming into our world change things? What would your relationship with God be like if God had not designed it this way?
- Consider thanking God for His love that compelled Him to send Jesus into our world.

DAY 19

DEVOTIONAL PASSAGE: LUKE 2:15-21

Here's the interesting thing about wonder: it forces us to make a choice. When we approach something with wonder, we open ourselves up to the curiosity of the moment. We are moved by the uniqueness or the grandeur or the overall awesomeness of what we see. But here's where the choice comes in. Once we marvel at the wonder of something, we must decide what to do with it. Do we tell others? Do we change our values or perspective? Do we stop and reflect on our identity or choices? Just being in awe of something isn't enough. We must consider what it means to be MOVED by our wonder.

Read Luke 2:15-21. The shepherds had an encounter with God's Kingdom in an amazing way. They wondered at what they saw. And afterward, they were left with a choice. What were they to do with the information they just heard?

The truth is that once we encounter Christ, each of us, you included, has a choice to make. We must respond one way or another. People will either move on this information, or they will not. They will either be compelled to know more, or they will choose to walk away. The shepherds had a choice. They made their choice, and they made it well.

The shepherds acted, and they retold. They heard, and they moved. They could have sat and talked, or they could have gone home. But they didn't. They followed through, and they were rewarded by coming face-to-face with the Son of God. Verse 17 says that once they were sure of the angels' message, they couldn't contain themselves. They started talking. They started spreading the word about Jesus. It was as if they couldn't keep quiet.

Today, over two thousand years later, we're still expected to do the same. If you know Christ, you should find yourself compelled to speak of His story. If you have encountered God and His Kingdom, you know that you will find it hard to keep your mouth shut. You have to move. You have to act. And with God empowering you, you will. And you'll be awesome.

THINK ABOUT THIS:

- What's keeping you from being a more powerful teller of Jesus' story? What can you do to be more committed to being someone who tells Jesus' story to others?

DAY 20

DEVOTIONAL PASSAGE: LUKE 2:8-20

The world can tend to make you lose your sense of wonder. We know it all, and we've seen it all. It's tough to slip something past us we haven't heard of before. While this isn't exactly true, we've been conditioned to feel like it is. With the prevalence of information at our fingertips, it certainly feels like just about everything worth knowing is available to be known.

And when we do see something we haven't seen before, we tend not to believe it's real. Do you see how easy it is to lose our sense of wonder? And that's a bad thing. Wonder is like curiosity times ten. It's the spirit of discovery. It's looking at the world around us with a healthy dose of "I can still be impressed, surprised, and amazed."

Read Luke 2:8-20. The shepherds had a huge sense of wonder. They had just been witness to a holy concert, a heavenly performance unlike any ever heard. And they were amazed. They were like, "Wow!" (Or something like that.) Moved by this, they took off running, acting on their strong sense of wonder, heading out to discover if what they had been told was true.

And, of course, they found that it was true. As true as anything could ever be. Their wonder was rewarded. They were amazed. Moved. Transfixed. All because they possessed an amazing curiosity and openness about God and His ways.

How is your sense of wonder?

THINK ABOUT THIS:

- What was the last thing, whether it was an experience or something you learned, that stopped you in your tracks and made you say, "wow"?
- Why is it so easy to just go through the motions of life, failing to have any wonder about the world around you?
- Can you know all there is to know about God? (Hint: no) What role does wonder play in knowing God better?

DAY 21

DEVOTIONAL PASSAGE: MATTHEW 2:1-6

If you think about it, we can define major moments in our lives by how we respond to them. When a problem arises, it's often not the problem itself that impacts us. It's how we respond to it. When an opportunity presents itself, the difference is whether or not you respond by seizing it or letting it pass you by. When you hear that a friend has let you down somehow, the relationship's future can often be determined by how you respond. When we look back at many situations in life, our response can either be seen as right or wrong.

Now, read Matthew 2:1-6. Here is the familiar story of the wise men. Now, you know this story. (But did you know that many people think that the wise men came to visit Jesus several months after He was born?) But I want you to look at it with fresh wonder. I want you to look at it with this concept of "reactions" in mind.

If you had to describe the wise men's reaction to Jesus, what words would you use? Curious? Inquisitive? Seeking? However you describe it, the point is that the wise men saw something in the stars that they regularly studied and rightly interpreted it as a sign that something spectacular had happened. Their response was the right one: they sought out Jesus, the King of the Jews. But look at Herod's response. How would you describe it? Calculated? Fearful? Power-hungry? Psychotic? Herod, the Roman-appointed ruler over this region, was a tyrant. And instead of being curious about the spiritual implications of Jesus' birth, Herod's response was wrong. He was scared that his power would be threatened, and he was fearful of who Jesus might be.

People still respond to Jesus in one of these two ways. They are either curious about who Jesus is and what He can do in and through them, or they are dismissive, fearful, or downright apathetic. Your life is a billboard for Jesus, and the way you live tells the world that you belong to Christ. People will respond to Jesus in you. And their response will either be right or wrong.

THINK ABOUT THIS:

- Are you responsible for how people respond to Jesus? What ARE you responsible for?
- How do you communicate the Gospel to the world around you? What are some examples of how you do this in your words? What are some examples of how you do this through your actions?

DAY 22

DEVOTIONAL PASSAGE: MATTHEW 2:7-12

What is worship? If you immediately thought about singing, don't worry: that IS worship. But worship is way more than praising God in song. Worship is one of those concepts we know when we see it, but that can sometimes be hard to put into words. I want to give you a definition of worship, which builds on our yesterday's discussion about responses. Are you ready for the definition? Here it goes:

Worship is a right reaction to an encounter with God.

Let's break this down a bit. First, think about when you encounter God. You can encounter God in the Bible, in nature, through prayer, by the conviction of the Holy Spirit, even through Christian community. And worship is simply how you respond to God once you recognize that you've encountered Him. Now do you see why worship is bigger than singing praise songs in church?

Read Matthew 2:7-12. The wise men didn't know exactly whom they would meet when they encountered Jesus. At least we don't think so. Based on the Bible, we know they expected to meet "the King of the Jews." But I am willing to bet they were surprised when they saw a young child in meager surroundings. Whether they were surprised or not, we can't say. But we can say this: when they encountered Jesus, they responded rightly. In other words, they WORSHIPPED! They gave Jesus the glory and honor He was due.

Let me ask you this: as you go throughout this Christmas season, are you looking for encounters with God? Are you expecting to encounter Him? Are you seeking places to sense His presence or see the works of His hand? You know, so much about our faith hinges on the idea of expectancy. We get too busy, especially this time of year. And we don't EXPECT to encounter God. When you do finally slow down enough to realize you're encountering God, be sure to focus on your response. Make sure you respond rightly, with worship to God for all He is and for all He has done. That's the best way to keep your sense of wonder toward God this Christmas season.

THINK ABOUT THIS:

- Today, simply be aware of where you may encounter God. Look for Him in the Bible, through prayer, in the world around you. Look for Him expecting to meet Him. And then respond with real, authentic worship.

DAY 23

DEVOTIONAL PASSAGE: LUKE 2:22-32

To be a person of wonder is to be a person who is open to being surprised. Have you ever been surprised by the faithfulness of a friend or family member? Hopefully, you have someone in your life who is with you through thick and thin, someone who is there when no one else is. For many of you, it will be a parent or grandparent. For others, it may be your best friend from school or church. No matter who it is, faithful friends are priceless. There aren't many blessings in this world better than someone who doesn't give up or give in.

As we get ready to wrap up this time of focusing on the wonder of the Christmas story, maybe it's good that we finish with this passage from Luke 2:22-32. Because this passage is all about faithfulness, it's all about not giving up or flaking out.

Read Luke 2:22-32. First, let's look at the faithfulness of Mary and Joseph. In this passage, we see them being faithful to the spiritual traditions of their people, the Jews. But more than this, Mary and Joseph have proven faithful throughout the entire story of Jesus' birth. They never wavered. And look at the faithfulness of Simeon! Simeon served day-in and day-out, waiting for the Lord to send a Savior. He never gave up. And he eventually had his faithfulness rewarded. Finally, God proved faithful in a variety of ways. He came through with His promise of a Messiah. And He was faithful in rewarding Simeon's service. Faithfulness is all over this story!

Faithfulness is one of the best qualities we can have. We model God when we demonstrate faithfulness. God is perfectly faithful in all His ways. And our call is to be faithful to Him. It's tempting to view our relationship with God as something we turn on or off depending on our surroundings. But faith doesn't work this way. Even though the road may be hard, we have to stay true to our faith in God. After all, God is true to us in every way, and it's the least we can do in return.

THINK ABOUT THIS:

- During this Christmas season, how have you seen your faith in God grow?
- Moving forward, what are some areas in your life where you could be more faithful in your commitment to follow Jesus?
- Say a prayer today asking God to remind you what it means to be faithful and to give you the strength to follow through.

DAY 24 Christmas Eve

DEVOTIONAL PASSAGE: LUKE 2:7

"And she gave birth to her firstborn son and wrapped him in swaddling cloths and laid him in a manger, because there was no place for them in the inn."

Read this and wonder ...

Can you imagine what that night must have been like 2,000 or so years ago? Imagine Mary, nine months pregnant, trying to find a place to stay the night. She had to know her delivery was close. Imagine the sounds and the smells of the stable in which she and Joseph finally hunkered down. And imagine what it must have been like to give birth to a baby in a barn.

What do you think was going through Mary and Joseph's minds? It's impossible to know for sure. But it's safe to say they were probably thankful, exhausted, relieved ... and maybe a little bit in awe. God had done what He said He would do. He promised a baby, and here he was.

I wonder if when Mary held baby Jesus' hands, she had any idea how those hands would pay the price for the sins of the entire world. I wonder if she dreamed of the fame and glory He would find on this earth. Do you think she had any clue how He would suffer for our sake?

We know the entire story. We have a benefit Mary and Joseph didn't have on that night. We can see those events in light of the rest of the story. But on that night, all Mary and Joseph knew was that God had sent His Son to be their son. And He had arrived. Safe and sound.

THINK ABOUT THIS:

- Tonight, as you read this, put yourself in that stable in Bethlehem so many years ago. Think about what it must have been like. Use your imagination. And prepare your heart to celebrate Jesus' birth.

DAY 24 Christmas Eve: Family

DEVOTIONAL PASSAGE: LUKE 1:5–LUKE 2:21

As a family, read the entire Christmas narrative as it's told in Luke.

FIRST, take turns reading from Luke 1:5–Luke 2:21.

THEN, when you've finished, go around the room and take turns sharing which parts of the story stand out as significant to you.

NEXT, take a moment and answer this question:

I am thankful God sent Jesus to this earth because _____.

FINALLY, consider wrapping up your devotion time by singing your favorite Christmas song(s) together as a family. Close in a prayer thanking God for loving us enough to send His Son to save us from our sins.

DAY 25 Christmas Day

DEVOTIONAL PASSAGE: ISAIAH 9:2-7

What a wonderful day to celebrate the birth of our Savior. With Jesus' birth comes hope, joy, and peace for all humankind.

This is a day to enjoy time with family and reflect on all that Christmas means to you. But before you do, read Isaiah 9:2-7, paying close attention to verses 6 and 7. You've read them before. They are familiar. But on this day, let their words sink in. Wonderful Counselor. Mighty God. Everlasting Father. Prince of Peace. Jesus is all of these things. And today is a day to celebrate God's decision to send Him into our world.

Enjoy this wonderful day with your friends and family.

DAY 25 Christmas Day Family

Here's a short devotional thought for you and your family on Christmas day.

FIRST, look at your Christmas tree. Have each person find an ornament that represents an aspect of the Christmas narrative. You may have some ornaments that are obvious connections to the Christmas story: stars, a manger, maybe even miniature nativity scenes. But it doesn't have to be literal. For instance, you might find an ornament of a toy; for you, it may represent the wise men giving Jesus gifts. Or maybe it's a cross ornament; this could represent Jesus and His birth. Whatever the case, take a moment and let each family member find an ornament that represents an aspect of the Christmas story.

THEN, take a moment for each person to share why they picked what they did.

FINALLY, when you've finished, have someone say a prayer for the family. Thank God for the gift of Christmas and all that it represents.

ABOUT THE AUTHOR
ANDY BLANKS

Andy Blanks is the Publisher and Co-Founder of Iron Hill Press and YM360. A former Marine, Andy has been doing ministry since the early 2000s, mostly in youth and men's ministry publishing and discipleship. During that time, Andy has led the development of some of the most popular Bible study curriculum and discipleship resources in the country. He has authored numerous books, Bible studies, and articles, and regularly speaks at events and conferences, both for adults and teenagers. He is active in his local church, teaching youth, adult, and men's small groups regularly.

Andy and his wife, Brendt, were married in 2000 and have lived in Birmingham, AL ever since. They have four children, three girls and one boy.

Graphic Designer   MORGAN WILLIAMS

Editorial Team   KERRY RAY + AMBER WARREN

Project Manager   HANNAH SOLOMON

YOU KNOW IT'S IMPORTANT TO GROW CLOSER TO GOD

YM360 DEVOTIONALS CAN HELP

Student devotionals from YM360 help you stay close to God by equipping you to creatively and relavantly dig-in to His Word.

CHECK OUT THE AWESOME SELECTION OF DEVOTIONAL BOOKS AT YM360.COM